Troubling Animals
on
Our Farm

Funny True Stories

Written and Illustrated by

Kinga Persson

Print information available on the last page

Rev. date: 06/16/2015

To order additional copies of this book, contact:
Xlibris
1-888-795-4274
www.Xlibris.com
Orders@Xlibris.com

Troubling Animals
on
Our Farm

Funny True Stories

Written and Illustrated by

Kinga Persson

I dedicate this story to all kids including my own

Lidia

Oliwia

Robin

This is my childhood house.

Introduction

When I was a little girl, I lived on a farm in a little wooden house. My mom was the boss of the farm with many types of animals and she knew how to deal with each of them. We played with them a lot, sometimes too much. Most of the animals were nice but some were unpredictable and would chase us kids when we were alone.

I grew up with two sisters and two brothers, but mostly, I spent time with my twin brother because my older brother and my sisters were in school. Kris and I were too young to go to schools so we acted like little monkeys, played and pranked all day alone. I remember there was not a single day without trouble involving our animals. Sometimes my sisters took part in the events. I will share some of the stories that I remember well and still make me laugh.

The ram running after my twin brother

The Thunder Storm and the Ram

It was a spring day. Nobody was home except my twin brother and me.

Each morning, we liked to jump through the bedroom window and climb the apple tree to eat the apples.

We didn't care about the thunder storm because we were having so much fun.

Suddenly, it began to pour rain, and the sky lit up with lightning, and thunder rumbled.

It scared my brother so much he jumped out of the tree and ran toward the house.

Hidden and waiting for Kris was the huge ram with curly large horns, running with his head down, ready to gore him.

Kris's face turned purple in fright, and his eyes almost popped out of his head. He barely got through the window with the ram right behind him.

I was still on the tree, I was laughing so hard I almost fell.

I couldn't come down from the tree because the ram was now waiting for me.

After a long time, my mom came home. The ram saw her and turned into a lamb. He was afraid of her.

The rooster on Jaga's head

The Bold Rooster

I remember we had one of a kind rooster who was so bold he would jump at you and take a ride on your head with his claws clinging into your hair.

One day, my friend Jaga came to play with me, and I heard her screaming outside the house, so I went to see what was wrong.

The rooster was on her head, clawing her. Jaga was frozen with fright.

I went out to shoo him away. When I did, the rooster jumped from her head and went after me.

He chased me into the kitchen, but when he saw my mom, he acted liked nothing happened and flew out of the kitchen as fast as he could. He was afraid of her.

Now we could play safely.

The dog getting my brother

The Tricky Dog

When you live on a farm, you have to have dogs to protect you and your house.

We had many dogs that I loved so much, except one.

My mom named the dog Loord because she likes unique names. He was submissive to her but was often teasing us.

When my mom left the house, she would chain Loord to his doghouse so he could not bite us while we were playing.

One day, my brother and I were playing hide-and-seek.

I was hiding, and suddenly, I saw Kris running away, and Loord was chasing him. Kris tried to escape from Loord by jumping on a nearby fence.

The dog jumped at him and snapped at his pants, pulling them down.

It was a funny sight, seeing the dog hanging onto his pants and my brother with a bare bottom hanging on the fence.

After seeing this, I also jumped on the fence to avoid the dog.

The dog finally let go, and we both started to laugh.

After a while, my mom returned home, and when Loord saw her, his tail curled downward, and he obediently left.

We were so happy.

My sister and I running away
from the bull

The Dangerous Bull

We had a bull on the farm. The bull was very strong and tricky.

During the summer, each morning, the cows and bulls must go two miles to the pasture to eat the grass.

One day, I went with my sister and mom to see how the bull behaved when we were with him.

On the way to the pasture, the bull pretended to be nice, but something was bothering him.

It was the red dresses my sister and I were wearing, because the color red makes a bull angry, but we felt safe because my mom was with us.

We got to the pasture and staked the bull so he could only go as far as the chain would stretch, and then we left him.

On the way back, we were having fun jumping and running, but suddenly, we heard a loud rumbling, and the ground started to shake.

It was the bull charging at my sister and me because of the red dresses.

We didn't know what to do. Luckily, there was a haystack in front of us, and we climbed quickly up to the top.

The bull was angry; he began butting the haystack to topple us down.

My mom came running to help us, and when the bull saw her, he froze.

Escaping from the horse

The Changeable Horse

We also had a horse on our farm. He was very handsome, and his coat was brown and shiny.

I rode him many times without a saddle, and sometimes I would fall, but I was never hurt.

The horse usually stayed in one place.

I remember the day I was feeding him a sugar cube.

He came to get the sugar from my hand. It made me very happy, and I talked to him of how much I loved him.

Suddenly, without reason, he got mad. He folded back his ears, and his eyes became wild, and he reared up on his hind legs.

I was so frightened my heart started pounding and almost exploded; my legs and whole body shook.

I started slowly backing up and escaped as fast as I could, but he started following me furiously.

The house door was wide open, so I ran with a full blast straight into the house and into the kitchen to hide.

The horse almost got into the kitchen, but my mom was there, and the wildness stopped.

My sister and the geese on her

The Silly Geese

If you see a flock of geese, it is better not to get too close because they well nip you.

The flock usually has a bossy gander, which can be very mean to children.

I think I was in kindergarten when my mom kept a large flock of geese, and they liked to hiss and chase us.

I remember a time when my sister was coming home from school, and when the geese saw her, they chased her around the yard, the well, and the trees.

She could not get to the house.

She was running around in circles with the geese behind her. The chasing went on so long that my sister got tired and gave up. When she did stop, the geese jumped on her back, pulling at her clothes and hair.

My mom came to rescue my sister just in time, and immediately, the geese just calmly left my sister. I was watching from the kitchen window, and I had divided feelings—run to help her or do anything.

I remember feeling sorry for her but also laughed at the same time.

The End

Although my stories are about some scary encounters with animals, our lives living with them was a wonderful experience. The scary moments are fun to tell about. In every episode my Mom was the hero that saved us.

I grew up on a small farm, nearby historic city Torun, where famous astronomer Nicolaus Copernicus was born. My siblings and I were influenced by the sublime pure atmosphere of my parental home. We were taught how to treat animals the right way; not to harm them, not to abuse and not to debase them. In 1994, I moved to Sweden to live with my Swedish husband, Mats Persson. In 1997, we moved to Mountain View (Silicon Valley), California with our three children. After ten years there, we moved to San Diego. By living in three different countries, I got exposed to multiple languages and cultures. My big passions are painting on canvas and making jokes. I love animals and I will always fight for their rights.

Printed in the United States
By Bookmasters